Junior Great Books®

READER'S JOURNAL

4 Trust
Resourcefulness
Communication

BOOK ONE

This journal belongs to:

The Great Books Foundation
A nonprofit educational organization

Junior Great Books® is a registered trademark of the Great Books Foundation.
Shared Inquiry™ is a trademark of the Great Books Foundation.
The contents of this publication include proprietary trademarks
and copyrighted materials and may be used or quoted only with
permission and appropriate credit to the Foundation.

Copyright © 2014 by The Great Books Foundation
Chicago, Illinois
All rights reserved
ISBN 978-1-939014-59-7

2 4 6 8 9 7 5 3 1
Printed in the United States of America

Cover art by Helen Cann.
Design by THINK Book Works.

Published and distributed by
THE GREAT BOOKS FOUNDATION
A nonprofit educational organization
35 East Wacker Drive, Suite 400
Chicago, IL 60601
www.greatbooks.org

CONTENTS

TRUST

1   THEME INTRODUCTION

3   THANK YOU, M'AM
Langston Hughes

11 CROW CALL
Lois Lowry

19 FRESH
Philippa Pearce

27 STORY-TO-STORY CONNECTION

RESOURCEFULNESS

29 THEME INTRODUCTION

31 SHREWD TODIE AND LYZER THE MISER
Ukrainian folktale as told by Isaac Bashevis Singer

39 **ON SAND ISLAND**
Jacqueline Briggs Martin

47 **THE GREEN MAN**
Gail E. Haley

55 STORY-TO-STORY CONNECTION

COMMUNICATION

57 THEME INTRODUCTION

59 **SONG OF HOPE**
Peggy Duffy

67 **JEAN LABADIE'S BIG BLACK DOG**
*French-Canadian folktale
as told by Natalie Savage Carlson*

75 **THUNDER, ELEPHANT, AND DOROBO**
African folktale as told by Humphrey Harman

83 STORY-TO-STORY CONNECTION

THEME INTRODUCTION
Trust

In this section of your book, you will read about characters who want to trust each other, or who are afraid to trust each other. Before you read these stories, think about this **theme question** and write your answer below.

How do you earn someone's trust?

_____
_____
_____
_____

After you read each story in this section, you may have some new answers to the question. Write them below.

_____
_____
_____
_____
_____

Reader's Journal 1

Thank You, M'am

by Langston Hughes

THANK YOU, M'AM

Sharing Questions

Write about **a part of the story that you understand better** after the sharing questions activity.

_____
_____
_____
_____
_____
_____

Write **the question someone else asked** that interests you the most.

_____
_____
_____
_____

THANK YOU, M'AM

Second Reading

Write **something new you learned** from rereading or from doing an activity during the second reading.

_____
_____
_____
_____
_____

Write **a question you'd like to talk about more**. It can be a question you thought of already or a new question. You can write more than one question if you wish.

_____
_____
_____
_____
_____

Reader's Journal 5

THANK YOU, M'AM

Head in the Clouds

Choose one of the topics in the clouds and write or draw a picture about it.

- All the things in Mrs. Jones's purse
- A picture of Roger's face when Mrs. Jones gives him the money
- What the beauty shop where Mrs. Jones works looks like
- Your favorite part of the story, and why

THANK YOU, M'AM

The focus question: _____

_____

_____

_____

Your answer before discussion: _____

_____

_____

_____

A piece of evidence from the story that supports your answer:

_____

_____

_____

Page: _____

Your answer after discussion (explain how you changed or added to your original answer):

_____

_____

_____

_____

Reader's Journal **7**

THANK YOU, M'AM

 Write your answer to the assigned essay question, and write three pieces of evidence from the story that support your answer.

Your answer to the assigned essay question:

Evidence #1 from page _____ :

Your evidence can be a quote from the story or a summary of what happens in your own words.

How this evidence supports your answer:

Explain how this piece of evidence supports your answer to the essay question.

8 Series 4 • Book One

THANK YOU, M'AM

Evidence #2 from page _____ :

How this evidence supports your answer:

Evidence #3 from page _____ :

How this evidence supports your answer:

> Use these notes to write an essay. Each main paragraph of your essay should give a piece of evidence and an explanation of how it supports your answer.

Reader's Journal

THANK YOU, M'AM

 Write a question you had about the story that still hasn't been answered. Use this page to take notes for a short story that answers your question.

Your question:

NOTES

BEGINNING: Where and when does this story happen? Who are the characters?

MIDDLE: What problems or important events happen?

END: Are the problems solved? What happens to the characters?

10 Series 4 • Book One

Crow Call

by Lois Lowry

CROW CALL

Sharing Questions

Write about **a part of the story that you understand better** after the sharing questions activity.

_____
_____
_____
_____
_____
_____

Write **the question someone else asked** that interests you the most.

_____
_____
_____
_____

Series 4 • Book One

CROW CALL

Second Reading

Write **something new you learned** from rereading or from doing an activity during the second reading.

_____
_____
_____
_____
_____

Write **a question you'd like to talk about more**. It can be a question you thought of already or a new question. You can write more than one question if you wish.

_____
_____
_____
_____
_____

Reader's Journal   13

CROW CALL

Head in the Clouds

Choose one of the topics in the clouds and write or draw a picture about it.

- What Kronenberg's window display looks like
- A time you were afraid of something new
- A picture of a crow taking care of its babies
- The character in the story you would choose to be, and why

CROW CALL

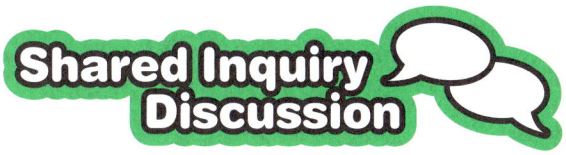

The focus question: _____

_____

_____

_____

Your answer before discussion: _____

_____

_____

_____

A piece of evidence from the story that supports your answer:

_____

_____

_____

_____ **Page:** _____

Your answer after discussion (explain how you changed or added to your original answer):

_____

_____

_____

_____

CROW CALL

 Write your answer to the assigned essay question, and write three pieces of evidence from the story that support your answer.

Your answer to the assigned essay question:

Evidence #1 from page _____:

Your evidence can be a quote from the story or a summary of what happens in your own words.

How this evidence supports your answer:

Explain how this piece of evidence supports your answer to the essay question.

CROW CALL

Evidence #2 from page _____ :

How this evidence supports your answer:

Evidence #3 from page _____ :

How this evidence supports your answer:

Use these notes to write an essay. Each main paragraph of your essay should give a piece of evidence and an explanation of how it supports your answer.

Reader's Journal   17

CROW CALL

Write a question you had about the story that still hasn't been answered. Use this page to take notes for a short story that answers your question.

Your question:

NOTES

BEGINNING: Where and when does this story happen? Who are the characters?

MIDDLE: What problems or important events happen?

END: Are the problems solved? What happens to the characters?

Fresh

by Philippa Pearce

FRESH

Sharing Questions

Write about **a part of the story that you understand better** after the sharing questions activity.

_____
_____
_____
_____
_____

Write **the question someone else asked** that interests you the most.

_____
_____
_____
_____

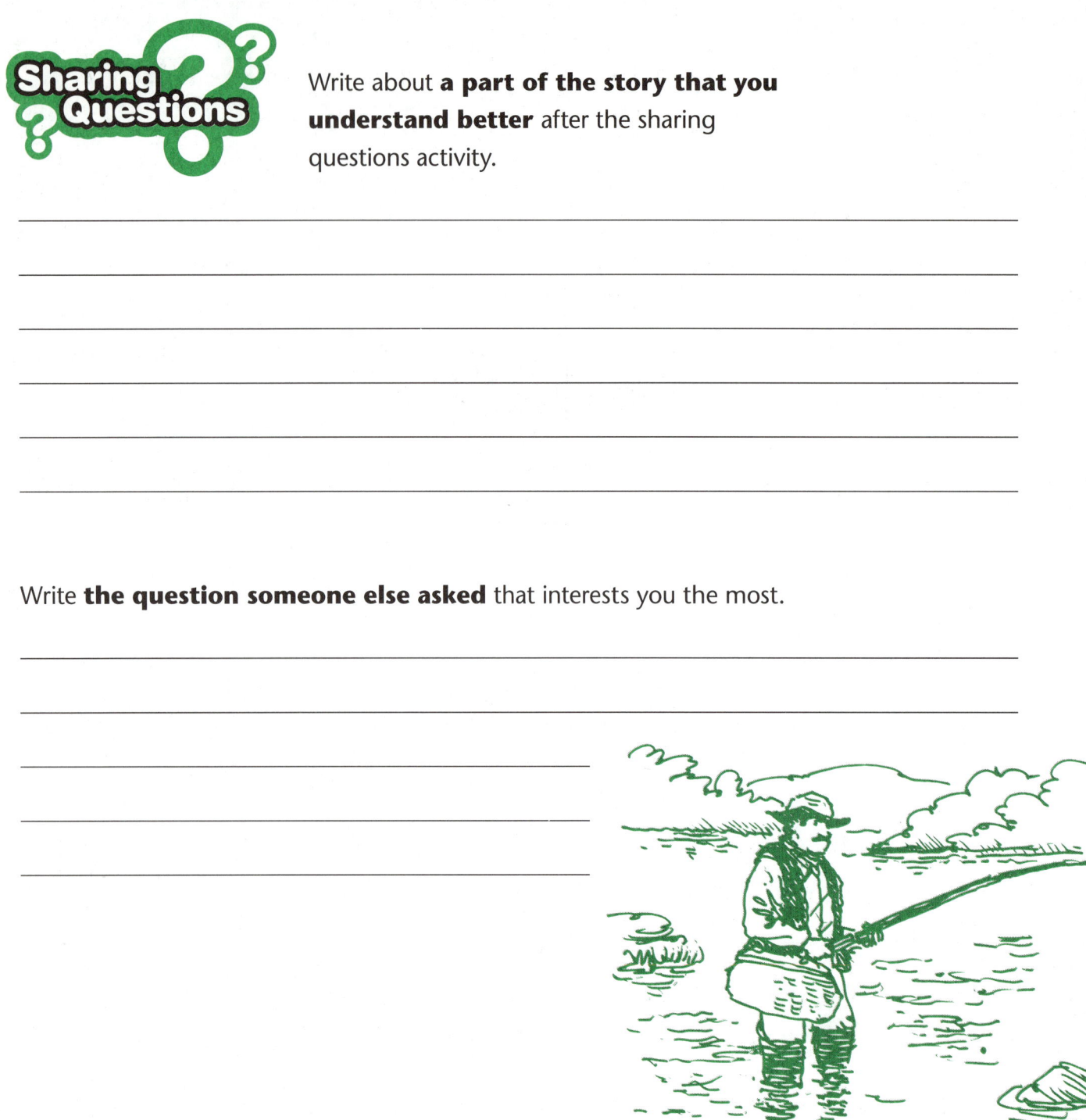

Second Reading

Write **something new you learned** from rereading or from doing an activity during the second reading.

_____
_____
_____
_____

Write **a question you'd like to talk about more**. It can be a question you thought of already or a new question. You can write more than one question if you wish.

_____
_____
_____
_____

FRESH

Head in the Clouds

Choose one of the topics in the clouds and write or draw a picture about it.

- A note from Dan to Laurie
- What Laurie's aquarium looks like
- A picture of Dan by the river at night
- A connection between the story and your own life

FRESH

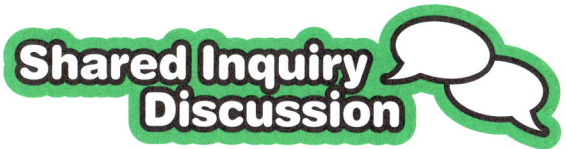

The focus question: _____
_____
_____
_____

Your answer before discussion: _____
_____
_____
_____

A piece of evidence from the story that supports your answer:
_____
_____
_____
_____ **Page:** ____

Your answer after discussion (explain how you changed or added to your original answer):
_____
_____
_____
_____

Reader's Journal   23

FRESH

 Write your answer to the assigned essay question, and write three pieces of evidence from the story that support your answer.

Your answer to the assigned essay question:

Evidence #1 from page _____ :

Your evidence can be a quote from the story or a summary of what happens in your own words.

How this evidence supports your answer:

Explain how this piece of evidence supports your answer to the essay question.

24 Series 4 • Book One

Evidence #2 from page _____ :

How this evidence supports your answer:

Evidence #3 from page _____ :

How this evidence supports your answer:

Use these notes to write an essay. Each main paragraph of your essay should give a piece of evidence and an explanation of how it supports your answer.

Reader's Journal 25

FRESH

 Write a question you had about the story that still hasn't been answered. Use this page to take notes for a short story that answers your question.

Your question:

NOTES

BEGINNING: Where and when does this story happen? Who are the characters?

MIDDLE: What problems or important events happen?

END: Are the problems solved? What happens to the characters?

26 Series 4 • Book One

STORY-TO-STORY CONNECTION
Trust

_____
OTHER GROUP MEMBERS

In each box below, write a **character trait** you think a person needs in order to be trustworthy. Then decide on a **story character** who has that trait. Write that character's name and a piece of **evidence** from the story that shows why that character has that trait.

Trait: _____

Character with this trait:
_____

Evidence from the story:
_____
_____
_____

Page: _____

Trait: _____

Character with this trait:
_____

Evidence from the story:
_____
_____
_____

Page: _____

Trait: _____

Character with this trait:
_____

Evidence from the story:
_____
_____
_____

Page: _____

Trait: _____

Character with this trait:
_____

Evidence from the story:
_____
_____
_____

Page: _____

Reader's Journal

THEME INTRODUCTION
Resourcefulness

In this section of your book, you will read about characters who find clever ways to get what they want or need. Before you read these stories, think about this **theme question** and write your answer below.

What does it mean to be resourceful?

_____
_____
_____
_____

After you read each story in this section, you may have some new answers to the question. Write them below.

_____
_____
_____
_____
_____
_____

Reader's Journal 29

Shrewd Todie and Lyzer the Miser

Ukranian folktale as told by Isaac Bashevis Singer

SHREWD TODIE AND LYZER THE MISER

Sharing Questions

Write about **a part of the story that you understand better** after the sharing questions activity.

_____
_____
_____
_____
_____
_____

Write **the question someone else asked** that interests you the most.

_____
_____
_____
_____

SHREWD TODIE AND LYZER THE MISER

Second Reading

Write **something new you learned** from rereading or from doing an activity during the second reading.

_____
_____
_____
_____

Write **a question you'd like to talk about more**. It can be a question you thought of already or a new question. You can write more than one question if you wish.

_____
_____
_____
_____

Reader's Journal 33

SHREWD TODIE AND LYZER THE MISER

Head in the Clouds

Choose one of the topics in the clouds and write or draw a picture about it.

- What you would say to Lyzer to convince him to loan you money
- What Todie's house looks like
- A picture of the townspeople singing their song about Lyzer
- How you felt at the end of the story

SHREWD TODIE AND LYZER THE MISER

Shared Inquiry Discussion

The focus question:

Your answer before discussion:

A piece of evidence from the story that supports your answer:

Page: _____

Your answer after discussion (explain how you changed or added to your original answer):

SHREWD TODIE AND LYZER THE MISER

Essay Organizer

Write your answer to the assigned essay question, and write three pieces of evidence from the story that support your answer.

Your answer to the assigned essay question:

Evidence #1 from page _____ :

Your evidence can be a quote from the story or a summary of what happens in your own words.

How this evidence supports your answer:

Explain how this piece of evidence supports your answer to the essay question.

SHREWD TODIE AND LYZER THE MISER

Evidence #2 from page _____:

How this evidence supports your answer:

Evidence #3 from page _____:

How this evidence supports your answer:

> Use these notes to write an essay. Each main paragraph of your essay should give a piece of evidence and an explanation of how it supports your answer.

Reader's Journal 37

SHREWD TODIE AND LYZER THE MISER

Story Organizer

Write a question you had about the story that still hasn't been answered. Use this page to take notes for a short story that answers your question.

Your question:

NOTES

BEGINNING: Where and when does this story happen? Who are the characters?

MIDDLE: What problems or important events happen?

END: Are the problems solved? What happens to the characters?

On Sand Island

by Jacqueline Briggs Martin

ON SAND ISLAND

Sharing Questions

Write about **a part of the story that you understand better** after the sharing questions activity.

_____
_____
_____
_____
_____
_____

Write **the question someone else asked** that interests you the most.

_____
_____
_____
_____

40 Series 4 • Book One

ON SAND ISLAND

Second Reading

Write **something new you learned** from rereading or from doing an activity during the second reading.

_____
_____
_____
_____
_____

Write **a question you'd like to talk about more**. It can be a question you thought of already or a new question. You can write more than one question if you wish.

_____
_____
_____
_____
_____

Reader's Journal 41

ON SAND ISLAND

Head in the Clouds

Choose one of the topics in the clouds and write or draw a picture about it.

- A time you had good luck
- A picture of Carl rowing his boat
- A picture of the celebration at the end of the story
- The character in the story that is most like you, and why

42

ON SAND ISLAND

Shared Inquiry Discussion

The focus question: _____

Your answer before discussion: _____

A piece of evidence from the story that supports your answer:

_____ **Page:** _____

Your answer after discussion (explain how you changed or added to your original answer):

Reader's Journal

ON SAND ISLAND

Essay Organizer

Write your answer to the assigned essay question, and write three pieces of evidence from the story that support your answer.

Your answer to the assigned essay question:

Evidence #1 from page _____ :

Your evidence can be a quote from the story or a summary of what happens in your own words.

How this evidence supports your answer:

Explain how this piece of evidence supports your answer to the essay question.

ON SAND ISLAND

Evidence #2 from page _____ :

How this evidence supports your answer:

Evidence #3 from page _____ :

How this evidence supports your answer:

Use these notes to write an essay. Each main paragraph of your essay should give a piece of evidence and an explanation of how it supports your answer.

Reader's Journal   **45**

ON SAND ISLAND

Story Organizer

Write a question you had about the story that still hasn't been answered. Use this page to take notes for a short story that answers your question.

Your question:

NOTES

BEGINNING: Where and when does this story happen? Who are the characters?

MIDDLE: What problems or important events happen?

END: Are the problems solved? What happens to the characters?

The Green Man

by Gail E. Haley

THE GREEN MAN

Sharing Questions

Write about **a part of the story that you understand better** after the sharing questions activity.

_____
_____
_____
_____
_____

Write **the question someone else asked** that interests you the most.

_____
_____
_____
_____

THE GREEN MAN

Second Reading

Write **something new you learned** from rereading or from doing an activity during the second reading.

Write **a question you'd like to talk about more**. It can be a question you thought of already or a new question. You can write more than one question if you wish.

Reader's Journal   49

THE GREEN MAN

Head in the Clouds

Choose one of the topics in the clouds and write or draw a picture about it.

- What it looks like inside Claude's cave
- Why you would or would not want to be the Green Man or Green Woman
- A picture of Claude riding in his fine clothes
- A note to one of the characters in the story

Shared Inquiry Discussion

The focus question:

Your answer before discussion:

A piece of evidence from the story that supports your answer:

Page:

Your answer after discussion (explain how you changed or added to your original answer):

THE GREEN MAN

Essay Organizer

Write your answer to the assigned essay question, and write three pieces of evidence from the story that support your answer.

Your answer to the assigned essay question:

Evidence #1 from page _____ :

Your evidence can be a quote from the story or a summary of what happens in your own words.

How this evidence supports your answer:

Explain how this piece of evidence supports your answer to the essay question.

THE GREEN MAN

Evidence #2 from page _____:

How this evidence supports your answer:

Evidence #3 from page _____:

How this evidence supports your answer:

Use these notes to write an essay. Each main paragraph of your essay should give a piece of evidence and an explanation of how it supports your answer.

Reader's Journal 53

THE GREEN MAN

Story Organizer

Write a question you had about the story that still hasn't been answered. Use this page to take notes for a short story that answers your question.

Your question:

NOTES

BEGINNING: Where and when does this story happen? Who are the characters?

MIDDLE: What problems or important events happen?

END: Are the problems solved? What happens to the characters?

STORY-TO-STORY CONNECTION
Resourcefulness

Fill in the chart below, using the stories to help you think about how each main character acted in a resourceful way. You will use this chart to help you act out scenes in class.

Character name	How the character is resourceful
Shrewd Todie	
Carl	
Claude	

TRY THIS

Choose your favorite scene that was acted out in class. On the next page, draw a picture or a comic strip of that scene.

THEME INTRODUCTION
Communication

In this section of your book, you will read about characters who find different ways to express their thoughts and feelings. Before you read these stories, think about this **theme question** and write your answer below.

What makes communication successful and what makes it unsuccessful?

_____
_____
_____
_____

After you read each story in this section, you may have some new answers to the question. Write them below.

_____
_____
_____
_____
_____

Reader's Journal

Song of Hope

by Peggy Duffy

SONG OF HOPE

Sharing Questions

Write about **a part of the story that you understand better** after the sharing questions activity.

_____
_____
_____
_____
_____
_____

Write **the question someone else asked** that interests you the most.

_____
_____
_____
_____

SONG OF HOPE

Second Reading

Write **something new you learned** from rereading or from doing an activity during the second reading.

_____
_____
_____
_____

Write **a question you'd like to talk about more**. It can be a question you thought of already or a new question. You can write more than one question if you wish.

_____
_____
_____
_____
_____

Reader's Journal   61

SONG OF HOPE

Head in the Clouds

Choose one of the topics in the clouds and write or draw a picture about it.

- A note from Tina to her coach
- What Tina's mother looks like while she watches Tina practice
- A picture of Tina playing soccer
- Two reasons why you like or do not like this story

62

SONG OF HOPE

Shared Inquiry Discussion

The focus question: _____

_____

_____

_____

Your answer before discussion: _____

_____

_____

_____

A piece of evidence from the story that supports your answer:

_____

_____

_____

_____ **Page:** _____

Your answer after discussion (explain how you changed or added to your original answer):

_____

_____

_____

_____

Reader's Journal 63

SONG OF HOPE

Essay Organizer

Write your answer to the assigned essay question, and write three pieces of evidence from the story that support your answer.

Your answer to the assigned essay question:

Evidence #1 from page _____ :

Your evidence can be a quote from the story or a summary of what happens in your own words.

How this evidence supports your answer:

Explain how this piece of evidence supports your answer to the essay question.

SONG OF HOPE

Evidence #2 from page _____ :

How this evidence supports your answer:

Evidence #3 from page _____ :

How this evidence supports your answer:

Use these notes to write an essay. Each main paragraph of your essay should give a piece of evidence and an explanation of how it supports your answer.

Reader's Journal 65

SONG OF HOPE

Story Organizer

Write a question you had about the story that still hasn't been answered. Use this page to take notes for a short story that answers your question.

Your question:

NOTES

BEGINNING: Where and when does this story happen? Who are the characters?

MIDDLE: What problems or important events happen?

END: Are the problems solved? What happens to the characters?

Jean Labadie's Big Black Dog

*French-Canadian folktale
as told by Natalie Savage Carlson*

JEAN LABADIE'S BIG BLACK DOG

Sharing Questions

Write about **a part of the story that you understand better** after the sharing questions activity.

_____
_____
_____
_____
_____

Write **the question someone else asked** that interests you the most.

_____
_____
_____
_____

JEAN LABADIE'S BIG BLACK DOG

Second Reading

Write **something new you learned** from rereading or from doing an activity during the second reading.

_____
_____
_____
_____
_____

Write **a question you'd like to talk about more**. It can be a question you thought of already or a new question. You can write more than one question if you wish.

_____
_____
_____
_____
_____

Reader's Journal

JEAN LABADIE'S BIG BLACK DOG

Head in the Clouds

Choose one of the topics in the clouds and write or draw a picture about it.

- A picture of the big black dog
- Something in the story that was funny
- What Jean looks like at the end of the story when he cries over the big black dog
- A conversation you might have with a story character

JEAN LABADIE'S BIG BLACK DOG

Shared Inquiry Discussion

The focus question: _____

_____

_____

_____

Your answer before discussion: _____

_____

_____

_____

A piece of evidence from the story that supports your answer:

_____

_____

_____

_____ **Page:** _____

Your answer after discussion (explain how you changed or added to your original answer):

_____

_____

_____

_____

Reader's Journal

JEAN LABADIE'S BIG BLACK DOG

Essay Organizer — Write your answer to the assigned essay question, and write three pieces of evidence from the story that support your answer.

Your answer to the assigned essay question:

Evidence #1 from page _____ :

Your evidence can be a quote from the story or a summary of what happens in your own words.

How this evidence supports your answer:

Explain how this piece of evidence supports your answer to the essay question.

JEAN LABADIE'S BIG BLACK DOG

JEAN LABADIE'S BIG BLACK DOG

Evidence #2 from page _____ :

How this evidence supports your answer:

Evidence #3 from page _____ :

How this evidence supports your answer:

> Use these notes to write an essay. Each main paragraph of your essay should give a piece of evidence and an explanation of how it supports your answer.

Reader's Journal

JEAN LABADIE'S BIG BLACK DOG

Story Organizer

Write a question you had about the story that still hasn't been answered. Use this page to take notes for a short story that answers your question.

Your question:

NOTES

BEGINNING: Where and when does this story happen? Who are the characters?

MIDDLE: What problems or important events happen?

END: Are the problems solved? What happens to the characters?

Thunder, Elephant, and Dorobo

African folktale as told by Humphrey Harman

THUNDER, ELEPHANT, AND DOROBO

Sharing Questions

Write about **a part of the story that you understand better** after the sharing questions activity.

_____
_____
_____
_____
_____
_____

Write **the question someone else asked** that interests you the most.

_____
_____
_____
_____

THUNDER, ELEPHANT, AND DOROBO

Second Reading

Write **something new you learned** from rereading or from doing an activity during the second reading.

_____
_____
_____
_____

Write **a question you'd like to talk about more**. It can be a question you thought of already or a new question. You can write more than one question if you wish.

_____
_____
_____
_____

Reader's Journal

THUNDER, ELEPHANT, AND DOROBO

Head in the Clouds

Choose one of the topics in the clouds and write or draw a picture about it.

- What Earth looked like when it had "only the things that *grow*" on it
- A piece of advice that you would give to Dorobo
- A picture of Elephant laughing and running from Dorobo
- Your favorite character in the story, and why

THUNDER, ELEPHANT, AND DOROBO

Shared Inquiry Discussion

The focus question: _____
_____
_____
_____

Your answer before discussion: _____
_____
_____
_____

A piece of evidence from the story that supports your answer:
_____
_____
_____
_____ **Page:** _____

Your answer after discussion (explain how you changed or added to your original answer):
_____
_____
_____
_____

Reader's Journal 79

THUNDER, ELEPHANT, AND DOROBO

Essay Organizer

Write your answer to the assigned essay question, and write three pieces of evidence from the story that support your answer.

Your answer to the assigned essay question:

Evidence #1 from page _____ :

Your evidence can be a quote from the story or a summary of what happens in your own words.

How this evidence supports your answer:

Explain how this piece of evidence supports your answer to the essay question.

THUNDER, ELEPHANT, AND DOROBO

Evidence #2 from page _____ :

How this evidence supports your answer:

Evidence #3 from page _____ :

How this evidence supports your answer:

Use these notes to write an essay. Each main paragraph of your essay should give a piece of evidence and an explanation of how it supports your answer.

Reader's Journal

THUNDER, ELEPHANT, AND DOROBO

Story Organizer

Write a question you had about the story that still hasn't been answered. Use this page to take notes for a short story that answers your question.

Your question:

NOTES

BEGINNING: Where and when does this story happen? Who are the characters?

MIDDLE: What problems or important events happen?

END: Are the problems solved? What happens to the characters?

STORY-TO-STORY CONNECTION
Communication

Two characters that would have a good conversation are _____

and _____ .

What they have in common (use details from the stories to support your answer):

_____
_____
_____

Now write a short conversation between the two characters about the thing that they have in common. Put one character's lines in the speech bubbles on the left, and the other character's lines in the speech bubbles on the right.